SOMETHING PRETTY

Poetry by Scott Benne

Something Pretty

A Divine Sammich Book / November 2006

First Edition

Published by Scott Benne

Florissant, MO

All rights reserved.

Copyright © 2006 by Scott Benne

ISBN: 978-0-6151-3666-0

ISBN: 0-615-13666-4

No part of this book may be reproduced or transmitted in any form or by any means without the written permission of the author, except where permitted by law.

for
Mike
Shorty

TABLE OF CONTENTS

Alley 1

Escape 2

Mine 3

Sip 3

Shade 4

Fill the Skies 4

And 5

Mist 6

Shrill 7

Beach 8

Fleeting 9

Wisp 9

Monumental Down 10

Beak 11

Flicker 12

Chirp 12

Mother 13

Crowned Courtship 13

Smooth 14

Bend 14

January 14

Fly 15

Lilies 15

Mouse 16

Squinting 17

Forgive 17

Mutiny 18

Submerged 19

Peels 19

Blue 20

Fountain 20

Former Glory 21

Mutter 22

Nonexistent 23

Tabitha 24

Obscure Birth 25

Boys 26

Muzzle 27

The Burn 28

Brother 29

Freedom 30

Trapped 31

Trance 32

Trigger 33

Canopy 34

Gateway Heart 35

Chicago 36

Collection 36

General 37

Her 38

Pant 39

True Power 40

Paw 41

God Bless This Mess 42

Out of Fear 44

Conception 45

Home Jest 46

Concubine 47

Jot 48

Invisible 49

Peak 50

Wade 51

Uncaring 52

Jimmy 53

Piss 54

Deeply 55

Prima Facie 56

Degrade 57

Dire Creation 58

Pretty 58

Laced 59

Midnight 60

Scratch 61

Member 61

You Venison 62

Launch 63

Ravage 64

pound 65

Conversation 66

Door 67

Dove Dive 68

Distraction 69

Down Time 70

Living Sacrifice 71

Rush 72

Dream 73

Ease 74

Mama 75

Sanctity 76

Erin 77

Mask 78

White Wash 78

Safe 79

Sanskrit 80

Lacking 81
Blanket 82
Wake 83
Red and Orange 84
Pristine 84
Crystal Castle 85

Alley

Half spent and more to gain

The wind whistling through the alley is a prison of fate

Only in that moment the sound exists

Then gone like the innocence of a tainted youth

Or the past, present, and future of an elderly saint

Directing his past transgressions on the suburbanites who troll about

Finding comfort in that which takes responsibility from them, not for them

Out in a thunderous spat

Clinging desperately like a banana in a trash bin

Or that little girl's mustard stain from a red themed burger joint

Where you aren't people but a potential statistic

Brick built this place and much like the alley is a place air goes to recycle and stagnate

Wild-eyed and on the floor

The dancing rats that feast on the money of the emptying middle-class

Scurrying about if the human remains of soul show a glint in the sidewalk

Blinded by the back light

The thumping rhythm in my chest shrieks shrill

ESCAPE

Airless thought

A dashing foot

Heat deep in your throat

Acid in your knees

Solid build

Up-hill nostalgia

The stolid memory

Silent and creeping

Sweat it out of your system

Trampling wormwood

Silk strands from spider hands

Tingle bare leg

No snow to mask your heave

However a ground with no remnants behind

The dagger lay stuck

Floor a disheartening final sleep

The first of all the etheric dreams

That you in a veiled life

Have experienced before

Creek, a splash

The snap of twigs and chanting

Hounds sparing no slack

Find the time

And leave behind

The service to some you have given

But for one the end of suffering

Mine

Tingle down my spine
Life in rewind
Future worries only a slurry
Expectations no longer alive
Deep and grueling
Government school
A job to succeed and a life you must lead
Or a societal fool
My dreams, though, exist where they belong
In poetry, film, and a lullaby song
The brand I see will have no marking on me
Liberty is my desire
A reality free

Sip

Sugar crystals line the foyer
Gently sprinkled from the inner workings of a coffee
Swirling in the dark
But pursing the lips so virtuous

SHADE

Roots beneath the ground
Bicycles gliding by
Butterflies set down
Flap symmetric
Blades of grass
Sight of the past
Buildings eclipse
Shadows with straight edges
Giggling and kissing under the juniper
Brisk and sunny
Wind without description
Newspaper fluttering by
Integral oasis to sanity
A standstill in a moving world

FILL THE SKIES

A dragon flies gracefully through the skies
In the clouds a sight like a white witch's spell
Its claws open and clamp grasping the air
A misunderstood creature not wanting to scare
Mystic being of plentiful beauty and size
Its emerald scales hypnotize

And

Pomp and circumstance
And a cradle dance
Cooing a dart through the dark
Piercing through the white wall
The dust that settles is churned
By a passing no slower than a blink

Pomp and circumstance
And a cradle dance
Throw the keys to the table
Peer up with a sting of shearing
Eyes that opened to the tears
Of a sacrificial lamb at the start

Pomp and circumstance
And a cradle dance
Beset the unlikely that me
Uniformly I, gazing at the knife
Woefully stick out my finger
Preparing for the battle to come
Confusion over a scheduled infinity
Had the world crossed my path
Or did I cross my eyes at the world
All I want is to make sure
Pomp and circumstance
And a deathbed chant

Mist

Rushing dexterity
Silence force beyond
White light illuminate
Link to my fate
Electric blue
Through my spine it flew
Warmth, a tickle
Heart and mind's eye
Fear set out to dry
Condensed and sent high
By the sun's loving kiss
Sprinkled in the leaves and beneath my feet
Teardrops of joy from an earth so pure
Ear to the ground
The purr of it all rejoices
Air is my savior and sight my blanket
Covering me from the dream
The experience set forward
Crashing the waves
The desert isle of my soul

SHRILL

Windowsill
She sat still
Come the chill
Sharpened knives
Idly she sat upon
His voice dulling the blade
Of waiting

One-sided coin
Confused, she flipped
Dedicated to a lie
He did not try
To find his way
Conscience frozen
Cooled by loathing
Tickle behind the ear
Truly it seared

He paid no mind
Agasp at a mirror
Sent away and left behind
Out the window
Of him reminded her
His true love in the dark
On the other a mark
Endless nights and bountiful frights

Breaking the glass
Was the only way
To remove their sight
And say goodbye

Beach

That washing sound and ducks in flight
Lake bed sprinkled in sediments
Man-made, a suburban oasis
Cut through by the state of the free vehicle
The kite flows vertical when the string is taut
Still from the ground yet spared second thought
Frisbee catch by the dog pawing the sand
The higher the heat, the more soothing a shadow
Wheat and almond butter stuck to my face
Smiling wide I am away from it all
Obligation, disease, electronic buzzing
The waves part and splash, unthinking
But more beautiful than any conscious entity

Fleeting

Wint'ry eyes
Muzzle flash
Ashes from a bare oak
Choke
Remnants of a shadow once
Only a slurry of thought
Is the truth that actually lies
Butterflies and sizzle
One to stop the other
Clasped at the wrist
Suddenly here, suddenly gone
If sacrificing nourishment
Would you fast your soul
A blanket to mask a history past
Relief melts without hast
In the dark of a hidden mem'ry

Wisp

Whip of hair
Do not despair
For the eyes you bury
Speak what words cannot

Monumental Down

The arbiter doughty
Lapse on melancholy
Translucent luster
Mandatory filibuster
Hammer gavel

You will travel home
Home is where the hard is
Your jailhouse cell
Eight by eight
A sharpened shiv's freight
Cinder block Hell
Final might the cell door spring
Gravel away from the sting

Intersection maunder
A life now flounders
Deep down the steep
Kicking your feet will topple you
Feet up-ended, dust pick-up
Counter balance
A hearty romance

You aren't you
But the tracing of a man once befitting
A rusted metal rocking chair you were sitting
When the whites of your eyes made me realize
There was nothing there but despair

Beak

On the telephone wire above me
A pigeon living with man
Made his place at home
As if a prisoner was content with his cell
I looked at him and understood
He saw the world in a way I could not
And similarly myself
Our eyes met only his nearly invisible
My static gaze made his aura glow
His feathers stopped with me
A blink would normally set them off
Skyward and out of sight
But in nature, we are brothers
Experiencing disharmony
An understanding between organisms
He twisted his head and slept

FLICKER

Burning dark
A being harp
Charring skin
A tenant's chagrin

Ash to the foot
Dancing footprints in the snow
Pattern-less show
Slow settle slow
Muddling my window

A wisp, a clatter
Transparent matter
Hover low
Chill the bone
Freeze from the inside out
My body shout
Throat turn a coat
And my chest ceases to throb

CHIRP

Lightning-fast twitch
Ride the slightest of gusts
A simple existence but one more interesting than my own

Mother

The rain stops
Came from once clouds
To glistening in the sunlight
If at night stars shine bright
Present at day
A bowed spectrum exudes
Nature changes at the whim of itself
Then one asks nature
Is driven by what magnanimous force
Knowing or believing answers set forth
But is it for us to know
The understated reality
Of all such things
Many questions wandered
Answered though remains at nothing
A climax of knowledge
Remains life's biggest paradox

Crowned Courtship

Sweet heiress
Crowned in the kingdom of my heart
She shall forever rule
As her just nature never wavers

Smooth

The air is painted by your grace
Flowing invisible an energy
Perpetual to the skin
Random particles
Yet the heart pounds with each pleasured breath

Bend

The cool slab was akin to a meat locker
Only I'd be alive and my muscles would remain intact
So the vegetarians have no way of revolting
The titanium drilled onto my spine would make me pro-lightning rod
I'd have no choice in the matter

January

The frost and crisp air outside my window
A night chilled from an artic front
Evidence of a preceding path
Obvious until the next snow storm
Although plants are dead, crystals are alive
Winter the brightest without the sun

FLY

Outside in the night
The moon glowing white
Shadow twice your size
Moths and June bugs soak up the sight
Clear as crystal and sparkily as such
Reach out your arms and stare deep on
Burning bright from million years gone
With no trees abound, off the ground
Witness infinity
Travel through time and find your way
The clouds on which you lay
Breathless and full
The ceiling alive and never-ending

LILIES

Steaming marshes
Spidery trees
Among the foliage
Lilies wade endlessly

Mouse

Ravens

Talons first and gates held stern

Beady eyes to terrorize

The scurrying pads of squeak and squander

Dig deep

Bury and carve

Wings flap gravely beyond reproach

Violence is seen when nature is splintered

For a blood lust only to see red flow

Among the beasts

Coda is mise en scene

Set up only by the morally capable

A distinct line however

Parted through dissidence

When a choice overcomes necessity

The great web is justified

As those who believe they are kings

Squinting

In grade school, I can remember ripping a blade of grass in half
The monotony of being disabled and listening to a gym teacher
Led to my bloodied thumb
I swept it over the organisms without a cardiovascular system
That betrayed my furry colony of cells
The skinny tomboy with pecan eyes narrowed her lids to slits
And hissed that I will find myself waiting for moist towelettes
Plus an all-inclusive three-hour stay at my resort from education
It seems soccer had an inherent advantage to the importance
Of finding a glorified piece of tape to soak up your red and whites
Goal

Forgive

There's a pain so deep
Beyond the bones and the hours of sleep
It looms and weathers
Binds with a tether
Walk over and stomp
Bloodied and softened up
Doing so wrong seems to be good
Or maybe doing things not as one should

Mutiny

Look outwardly and you will see
Things are not as they seem to be
The quickest response, a passionate event
Is easier to digest without complexity

Ockham's razor tells me so
The response time to reality
Is radically slow
I sit and I stew and I sweat
Wagering money on my own bet
Fearing the worst, expecting the most
A palpitating heart is what you get

Calm yourself down with words of reason
Don't step outside your boundary
That's treason
To think and to say means nothing without do
Do sets in motion what you thought you knew
Uncovering the contents of your hidden self
Is merely hanging on to what's been known before
A past you hide so well, it's lore

Before you riot, setting forth mutiny
Think for two minutes and you will see
Things are not as they seem to be

Submerged

Submerged
Deep into the almond strands
Carried is my gaze
Into the starry blue

An open window
To what warmth covers her
Admiring from afar
But not afraid to touch
What is inside

An astral projection
Only injected into reality
The grace that illuminates
A love worth not having

Peels

Stunning vistas of the sky
Matching the dynamic glow
The tingle on my lips
A citrus show

Blue

I see you
Triumphant blue
Avoiding suffocation
From an unyielding hue
Green to be
All I see
It's you I need
My heart you lead
Dance the floor
Light through the smoke
Pink in the heart
Evoking no choke

Fountain

Water droplets
Returning to its source
Gravity grabs it

Looks like remorse
Tears dripping freely
In a cement reservoir

Former Glory

Drip boundless there
The puddles and muck
Down prances the pony
Up forces the draft of replenishment
Dripping still by beaded relief
If not for the frigid air

Coolly pounded the colorless lay
Underneath my foot
Pattered and pounded next to plastic
Laden with sugar and calories
Looking up in the endless bevel

The dress of milady dangling free
I loved her once
Yet she not me
Boorish it seems
Only momentary self-loathing and then
The glory of all

Raw, unwavering, held stern in the soft
Hold the door and pretend to be
Formerly fulfilling in a burrow of arms
Only now down to nostril and cry
Inside she deeply longs for I

Muttered

Release the tension
Haste me to mention
Depths of melancholia
Is my prose of wanton purge

Written seldom
Are whims of superlative
I have time for dark whimpers not
In a life I find contentment
Among those who comb the sands
For the toothpick of a foe-like no-goody
Constantly

When will the angry mob stop
And see what their flames illuminate
If shadows be among us
The entirety of the selected front
Is nary to be completely seen for all its worth

Sprinkling rain water is a shelved observation
Something so obvious yet thought to be secret
Tears at my ear
Like the screeching end of a sewer rat

Angry I am
At her or I incomprehensible
I shout out
Clout
But my screams are sheltered in my chest
For the vibrato stir
Does nothing but shiver the spines of those who take no joy
In what we trample past
To the end of dusk

Nonexistent

The floor cracking beneath my wheels vindicates the termites
I am three weeks before being four weeks late
It's only a goal so I can have something to float by
The necessary evil of electricity opens my back door
Hitting the deck in the eight o'clock chill makes my feet seem to weep
The chlorophyll filters the energy in a blue shadow across my face, much like my thoughts filtering into dreams
The gentle fog makes a dreamscape seen in scrambled eggs
I let go of my net and find beauty in the connection
The air conditioning and cardinals have the same value with my eyes closed
I choose to forget about them
Clawing out of her perch and sending me back, the bitch is blue
The world is asleep when it wakes up
Tendrils of the boasted sunlight blind or brighten

Tabitha

Red overcoat

Rain drops splatter and set

Jump a puddle to land in another

The sirens singing

Bullets flow and beaming

Face down

Too late to drown

Trickling away from the abdomen

Ephemeral without wrinkle

But stretched too long in life

The trolley slows and shouts are gleaming

The hot muzzle's continual steaming

Offered a rock the man drops hard

Magnum slapping on slick cement

Repent, lament

Beyond he'd sent

Crackle, clatter, dirt smatter

Clipped

All made to be enemy

Trust an antique buzz word

Where had it gone

Burning gas tanks and crumbling building

Stood up
Jay-walking a lawless street
Pattering of feet
The man on his knees rolls her over and sees
The smile not wiped from her lips
Once a man slips
His lesson worth the shot

Obscure Birth

The dreams beyond a harmonic song
And the clouds sweetly hanging above
The are things you can know of love
If all you ever do is long

The trees sway and move the shade
Blades of grass come to pass
The falling kite of a lass
To which her brother pointed and laid

Look above, don't you see it?
He gleefully bellowed
The lass of seven peered high

The expression of her face further mellowed
Against the freshly fallen leaves to sit
The dove in the heavens made her cry

Boys

Is it a man to drink and shout
Join in the communal, trivial joust
Or is it a man to accept within
Emotional distraction is commonplace throughout

Fag and a queer
Swallow down the beer
Soon you'll be clear
A stag and a steer

Out of their mouth an ignorance frequent
If you walk a different path
Bequeath on them the judgment at hand
Their messages lost as if high tide over sand
Forgetting themselves, their lives are shelved

Feeling one without a finger lift
The rules of femininity start to shift
They follow suit
And the true masculine
Is a shark without a fin

Real men have lost
To the ego, libido, and desire
No longer the shape of the wave
Is how man should not behave

Muzzle

Vodka rocks
Diluted shots
Burn away
Handing my force
Misanthropy at sea
Where all alone
I escape the livid
Produced only
By my eye's mind

A wave of warmth
Splash my septum
I long for the dizzying comfort
Muzzled only by a cap
Slip
Twist off

Inside I need
Only the fee
Of a mild poison
Take me away
Oh
Away I take myself

The Burn

Speared residence
No hesitance
Spare precedence
Surface to air
Treasure chest
Dirt and debris
Mercury sea
Orange cloud flee
Burning up
Turning up
Downtrodden it
Drained bog sit
Merciless
Those turbulent
Scream and shout
Flipping out
Holding you
Turn a clue
Eagle flew
Side road
Rock erode
Bouncing round
Slamming sound
Dreaming to escape
Living to return

Brother

In three weeks time
These tears of mine
Will be over you

When you were five
Your eyes were alive
Because giants were true

Now you see what life can be
Without a complaint
Your emotions are quaint
And remorsefully I let you go

Not out of sadness do I feel this way
In your presence I've nothing to say
My respect for you has never gone
If I was a singer I'd write you a song
I'd make it a hit to send out the message
Daily on the radio you'd know how much I'll miss you

I already do and have for so long
In my heart is where you belong
When you step out of sight
And disappear into a field
My love for you will never yield
My beautiful baby brother

Freedom

Interaction.
Subtraction.
Master reaction.
Don't you think
That all of this stink
Is part of the little
That makes up the rest?

The thing that surprises
Beyond the surmises
Is the utter importance
Of every little thing
That makes up the whole
That allows us to sing.
Why do we sing?
To bring all together
(Another tiny thing)
Like birds of a feather.

Maybe,
Just if,
We are all together,
Bound by the air we're around,
Tied by the atoms and kept whole by the spin,
We're allowed to sound,
To vent and deceive.

To know we are free
Is most comforting.
Part of a whole but no more less,
Looking beyond the box is what I suggest.

TRAPPED

Bane, chain, driving me insane
But even this literal rhythm
The simple unchanging click
Questions the complexity
Of this world

Hate, fate, coagulate
Why must blood boil under pressure
If the only emotion it's good for
Is pain, peril, and anger
All too commonly

Rock, clock, binding lock
The only constant is time
And even existence is a fraction
When on this planet
There's no escape

TRANCE

True to the touch
Vacant to the nerve
Find me wandering
No longer will I serve
A rhyme, a scheme
Long-winded rules to press

Defined our lives are not
By a pattern known to all
The words through my fingers
Hardened with instinct
Blind to all else
But ease into adoration

Would the writing survive without me
Or will I be lesser for caging passionate pursuits
Obvious some would say
This poem from a constant presence

Speak up
Choke it out if you must
Are your senses tingled by the color of the pen
Or the moments between the strokes
I beg you
Pleading for your warmth

I crave to be seen by the ignorance
Disposition
Anyone at this moment
Loneliness will recede

TRIGGER

Nodule under my skin
Where do I begin
A lump in the throat
Or the remnants of a hardened heart
Black like a cancerous lung
Everything can be unsung
If it hastily finds itself eroding
Behind a forgetful eye
A tempted fate squeezed from thought
An elephant in the room
Finds its way to doom if the scolding tip
Of a fired rifle steams in the rain
Don't drench me yet or sink my foot below the horizon
Finding yourself in entrenched mud
Is an extravagant release
Down I go past the millions of fore-bares
Do twice the eyes see my descent
Or am I only lying to myself

Canopy

Do I feel clandestine to the touch
Is my love too much
Searing inside your mouth
Your heart wanted to break free
Hold it down beneath the water on your brain
Being happy is pretty plain
Change is a progression for the better
My head can wrap around the bend
Signals do not send
Through the air thick with haze
Progression to amaze
Are my hands urging you west
Over mountains and the streams
Drowning in the figs
Climbing on the water
Suddenly I feel amassing increments
The dirty innocence
Getting you right makes you mewl
Dragging down the path
Purging away the fantasy of a hidden realm
Your shoulders at the helm
The beating in my chest screeches for you

GATEWAY HEART

Ardent euphoria
Pulsing through my arteries
Benevolent persona
Forcing one to their knees
A gasp of entrance
When air transposes want
Creature of fate benign
Or is it truthful shunt

Beauty lies behind the eyes
And not on the surface fervently
Love lies behind the guise
Of a sheen placed so delicately
Transcendent gaze
Entering my spirit adorn
One moment without haze
Where passion tools and lays

Beauty lies behind the eyes
And not on the surface fervently
Mindful though find the skies
As the oasis of idolatry
Love lies behind the guise
Of a sheen placed so delicately

Chicago

Human ingenuity
Sent skyward briskly
Sitting on what could be the sea
Small but significant
A bud on a sequoia
Welling up
I felt free

Collection

Water dripped on my right shoulder as I stood squarely in a circle

Our hands were grasped like prisoners making their way across a river when the scaffolding betrayed the gun tower

We protested not protesting

I didn't realize if people wanted to watch paint dry, they'd get a brush and a dip it in red

Getting looks for not doing anything in particular was discouraging for the athletes

Business meetings followed by two seconds of terror was their drug

The flag was at half-mast for a full-fledged bastard

I didn't notice

I guess we protested the sky too

GENERAL

Closing my eyes
Rhythm of the bass
Shock wave
Throw my hands up
Let it out
Soul embrace

You complete stranger
Sing passionately
Like you wrote the words
The coursing cloud
Sandwiching in
Battle scar healed
Face awash
Drenched to the toe

Never leave
We all belong
Paths converging on the dirtied floor
Set indefinite
Frenzied cat calls
Dignity retract
But needlessly they are lost

Bellow the chord
Thumb the six string
Your words though not always spoken
Are the longest lasting imprints
To know you are not alone
Is the greatest victory

Her

Long I gaze into the timeless
A sparkled gold in a forested green
Berating null
Fingertips dashing through

Temple wet of passion
Sheen of tangle delicately thrown
Soft of pink
Lips grabbing hold
Pulling inward fine

Here I lay
Where there is no time
But even then
Infinity seems lacking

Pant

Surface glee inexorably
Legs hiked noticeably
Inverted tulip and shoe
Gray streak gracefully strewn

Woman of middle age may be my sage
Rolling up and down curve and hip
Certainly physical through lacking options
Revel in it, however, I certainly do

Too much too soon
Too little to judge but much to watch
Advice that works from an idiot box
Down to the floor but opposite to socks
Italian, raised and cloth

It's an illusion as my open eyes glance
I enjoy the trance
The spectacle of she
Magic among a burning Rome dance

True Power

Those grenades that you lob
Cause all the mothers to sob
And victims to exact revenge
The Hell man created
Leaves courage baited
And hope a lost memory

It takes more of a man
To take a shrill stand
Against those who revel in agony
Fight back with your mind
Push fear and sadness behind
'Cause love can't be defeated

See what you've done
With the barrel of a gun
Are you not a sinner?
Question what you see
If not, all that will be
Will be mongered on t.v.

Be with us or against us
But far from the fronts
Either way you aren't an enemy
The craters they left
Life taking's a theft

Leave them with no moral fiber
The world is not over
Get clean and get sober
And exalt liberty

Paw

Moonlight and shadow caressing my skin
Purple mountains let me in
Among the burrows behind the trees
I found cold comfort among the leaves
Drenched in fear, running from sweat
The thistle pressed against me
Howling, the coyotes search and stumble
Fur up and down a tangled mange
The rotting cedar log and the noises beyond
Mud in my fingertips neighboring a slug
Where have I ran - how far have I gone
Valley below sparkling crystal suburb
Lincoln Street north of the square
They were sleeping unaware
Snap and clamor falling hard
Pant leg rip and a future scar
This game is too much
Increasing my isolation I do
Limp home like a wounded coyote
Yelp to calm in arms of family

God Bless This Mess

Assimilate your forces
Transform love to hate
Rise your guns and cannons
Rush through the gate

Apply pressure to the vein
The limb will turn red
Take no prisoners
We went the innocent dead

In bold news titling
We want it to read
Families Will Die
For Us To Succeed

If they bite at us
We can bite back
The rules of engagement
Hide our attack

The lie is peace
By means of violence
If people disagree
Maintain your innocence

Behind a waving flag
We must unite
Blood letting must be
A common sight

Scare them and numb
Their senses with fear
Money for college
And endless beer

Come on, come all
Join the fight
Murder for hire
Do what is right

Stand fast for slavery
That is what it's about
In the middle of the desert
We can ignore their shout

So go on boys
Our souls are long gone
Let the leaders take over
By dropping the bomb

Out of Fear

Short of dreams, long on stillness
The air encapsulated in my lungs
Deep and resounding a rhythmic rush
Tingle through the palms
Thinking of the place where all can be
Eyes shut tight to the dancing gray flutter
Purple amoebas spring about
Feeling the body but known to be out

Deeper still, falling in breath
The blackness extending long past abysmal
Rush of nothing and a shock to the center
The comfort transforms to a tunneled energy
Three dimensions no longer seen
Shaking, pounding, squeezing through
Stop

Gliding and glistening
Silver tunnel as large as a sprout
The forehead entrance
Immobility
Resemblance to someone known
Itself the bed indents the body with
A success

Alive and well in that place unknown
Free from the mind itself
Found from a spirit on the shoulder
Bed body springs salty response
Eyes glisten clear
Fright and fear fading away
The beauty of it all will always remain
Go back and taste what others naught
Your world is an illusion long forgot

Conception

Fresh to conception
Stance of the martyr
Carrot chopped to feast our stomach
Umbrella draining the rain
Lore to the Scotsman
Rock back and fro
Trees glisten lime
Golden rays above
Gray would cripple it
Nailed through a creaking floor
Snow far below
Tiling the backward pattern
Pink upon the wall
Hospital food as a last resort

Home Jest

The beach long and winding
Ebbing water at the moon's pull
Silence gracing the color green
Feeble attempts at warmth from a dying fire
In her eyes, a minute flicker
Behind her mind the moon glowed full
Drinking down the vodka
Shifting her hair from her eyes
She was beautiful
We were homeless
Three months on and she still shook
Wondering why her life lead to sand pillows
An uncommon Carolina chill
I found myself free
No bills, no need to mop, no need to remove trash
The dog slept soundly
More comfortable that she ever was on hardwood
Am I lazy or have I lost the grasp of material?
My shirt was stained in mustard
During a fight over finances long ago
Her eyes pierce my mind
Inside hating me but also knowing it's for trivial reasons
Passed out from half a bottle, I gave her my comforter
I ran through the night thinking and warming up
When I returned, it was time to move with the tide

Concubine

Enticed by the air you release
My body did not scream for police
I found myself craving your life
But instead I held a knife
To my chest, for what my heart
Wanted it did not receive
I did not deserve you I once thought
Until my lust for you was bereaved
I was a five dollar whore for a four dollar man
A paper doll dangling from the cutter's hand
You loved me for what I did for you
Without a spigot of guilty burn

I loved you for what you gave me
A feeling of belonging like a pebble in sand
Until you sliced me open, down to my knees
My heart, your siege, my youth, your disease
You might as well have done me in
What is worth feeling you're the one with sin
Cut from the tracings of stunted fingers grown
White washed my face and I was alone
It was me all along, wasn't it
For your love must have been worth my pain
My naivety was all the purpose to regain
The stinging kiss of the back of a hand
Hurt me so, I won't do it again

Time heals all wounds but doesn't soak up
The blood-stained wood underneath the carpet
A thin line of jagged skin I tear into my arm
What's the harm? I was cut and pierced and prodded
More than I could do on my own
For my only release was not easily sewn
Back together, cut-outs can't be saved when burned

It's the present day now and I have now seen
All the clippings in my actions to piece together
I was rich inside for a worthless hand
You are merely a footprint in the sand
You are gone when I turn my back
But I may never shake
How much of a glue you lacked

The knife is a symbol of your stabbing eyes
But like all things, it has dulled with time

Jot

I took a bite out of the flavorless words
Down poured an emotion that came out slurred
A shift of my hand and a rise to my face
I ate until I was full of haiku and propaganda
Both of which end up the same in the end

Invisible

Blowing breeze
Tell me please
Do you bring life
Or carry disease
Wind on my face
Can't be the case
When through the air
Leaves can't find their place

Carried are the dead
Of insects and trees
The floating paper is said
The world is full of pleas

Can't get in my head
The end is the seas
Silent movement is fed
By nature's fees

But life as a constant
And not for an instant
Does it stop for man
And life at its hand

Transparent breeze
Thick of the seas
Winds can mourn
Life can reborn

Peak

Would rain be as refreshing
If oil traveled down the sloping ground
Polluted yet we still step through it
Ignoring what is emerging between our toes
Until you are face-down in it
If I breathed it in
Would I be alright
But a substance so deliquescent
Makes the footing unbearable
Is the only comfort
In the water that rids of us our grime
Or can our skin protect
From the black mass infecting

WADE

In chaos comes beauty
In the stagnant comes bore
Mind is the water
Limits are the shore
Graceful and elegant
Keeper of life
Two feet on land
The stressor of strife

The simple complexity
Of waves crashing in
Have all the potential
To wash out your sins
Wrongdoing is not
What the fearful despise
It's what makes you feel
Like you're missing your life

Inside us all
Is a potential for godliness
Live like you would
For nothing less
Put one toe in
And make yourself at home
Nature provides
Even when you are alone

The ripples won't happen
If you provide no rock
Shake up your mind
And ready for a shock
You control the waves
And life is your sandbox

UNCARING

Venial tact
Leaves no excuse
When the body and mind
Destroy each other
Open up my capacious wound
Barely threaded
By the stitches so desperately clinging
Ride the edge of certitude
With a busker
Ill-treating you not
Emblazoned with a name
You trust with repose
Must I mind a beaten direction
If it musters uncaring
When I part its dust
For that is all it knows

Jimmy

James or Jim
Your face to the floor
Formally and formerly sound the same
Not by vocal thrust

Knee, total collapse
Saliva drip
Slow-motion slip
Sweet poison
Bounty for a dollar
Deaf enough to see
Hardly blind enough to hear

Running joke
Serial laughing stock
Bourbon poured in a cracked glass
The dust collected

Shoe, they need the cleaning
Jimmy, pick up your phone
Leave a message
I'm numb

Piss

Piss
Do you see my face
Look up
Do you see her grace
Fuck up
Let her go
Sit down
Go to you
Hit sound
Smack
Splinter my ears
Scream my fears
Roar
Snore
Human boar
Reticulate in my filth
Impervious to my wit
Sit
Shit
Nowhere to stand but sideways
Crack the spackle
Skull trash
My shoes erode
Disparaging load
Breathe beneath the smoke
In three inches of water

Deeply

I shuffled through the crowd
Tip-toeing with martini in hand
Ice floating, olive slowly
Moving in the glass

She stood there lean
Dress draping softly on her thigh
Lips pursed and hand on side
I was barely breathing
Constricted and bonded
I hardly noticed when the elbow hit me

The drink a waterfall without a precipice
Falling together and staining the carpet
A smirk, a giggle
Glancing to her eyes

I needed another and I needed her
I left the puddle and headed forth
Bartender, I need a paper towel
What I want I already have

Held my wife's left hand
And dreamed deeply body to body

Prima Facie

Your glowing face
And warm embrace
Is all the motivation
I need to chase
Your heart

Starry eyes
Soft thighs
Lips and kisses that hypnotize
In my arms you remained
Time itself went untamed

Our moment together
Fleeting and special
Being found out
Lowered our threshold
To handle our pain

I hold at my chest
Your writings on note paper
Folded up
So the corners don't taper
Hidden in my drawer

When you came into view
With your green jacket and jeans
Tears didn't come
It seemed untrue
But far apart, I still miss you

DEGRADE

Sprout through the ground an A-list shroud
Your roots dig deep like one of the crowd
Immobile and sunk deep into the earth
Fire and wind, punished like you sinned
Burnt and shoved you rose above
And stood there ever motionless
Throughout the years among the leers
Of those who stand in awe at your base
Leaves covering your face
Hidden from view a lewd avenue
Long summer nights of charred barbecue
The howl of the invisible mass
Toppled you at long last
During the foreboding ravages of an angry cloud
The clap of thunder frighteningly loud
Find your path beneath the ground
Nutrients deep in clay
Standing still you forget your voice
But now there's nothing to say

Dire Creation

His brass flask glistened on the side of the road
Hitchhiking drunk confused the drivers who went by
He couldn't walk a straight line
I was parched
"Sandpaper in the Mojave" I penciled into my note pad
I didn't dare down the diluted poison
I never handled the stuff well
My common sense told me that drinking in the middle of a desert would dry me up
"Quicker than beads of a sweat on a salt plain"
Eventually the predictable happened
I walked over to check how badly his leg was broken
Looking at the flask, I was tempted
But looking at the idiot on the shoulder
Changed my mind in a hurry
"Crap"

Pretty

Off with their head
Better off dead
I know you're a liar
So spit out that fire
Your scales are searing off

Make up your mind
Are you on the outside
A burden so heavy
Bursting that levee
Dowsing what melts your lead

My heart has been split
The furnace is lit
You are now illuminated
For what you really are

Laced

Industrialized
Silk socket
Enclosing the contents
From a rich pick-pocket

Expertise in money-making
By launching off a rocket
Marketing it all
For a way to solve the act of sinning
But nobody's winning

Post-trauma or post-mortem
In the rubble many sort them
Level the playing field

Only a school
Firing off a tool soaked in blood
Boots through the mud
Tracks hidden away silently

Midnight

Electrical dance when I open my eyes
It reminds me what is
Five senses ground us
Energy bodies that play tricks
Dark makes my surroundings a polluted-snow
Or maybe the sun alters
I don't rely too heavily on either
An illusion interpreting
My eyes cloudy
Survived an attack by petroleum jelly
Oils preventing my full capabilities
I see clearer sleeping anyway
Nod off and pain subsides
Dream awake

Scratch

Mountain and earth beneath the street
High and beyond screams defeat
Material gone so what's left
Not a theft
But the removal of doubt
Body a vehicle
A pound of flesh and six of brain
Questioning theism seems insane
In a positive way
Not even that
A park bench riddled in dirt she sat
Jeans torn and scars at the forearm
Deceitful world
Portal to thinking on a broad scale

Member

Graceful monarch butterfly
Complementary against the sky
Flying low, I let out a sigh
Sight of symmetry made me cry
Incapable of a lie
It flaps its wings by
A denizen of the sky
Back to the clouds it flies

You, Venison

Piper on the street
Run, fly, bounce
Fawns I can not see but believe they exist
The only few I've seen may be the only there is
Tell me you've seen them
Sighted them silky

Tell them, piper
We are the only two to witness this deer
With your own two eyes
Is conclusive
With a million more you still need a look
If t.v. is a lie and the papers are owned
Trekking five feet to see what is real
Is less than a fired shot
For spud root and venison
I eat but have never seen

I trust a fawn to be downed and fed to my mouth
Fascination draws me in
But I'm no hurry
To know what is real and expel what myth
That exists entrenched

Piper, sing them a song
They need to go outside

Launch

Crescent shapes

Scarlet traipse

Dizzying array of a cavalcade

Hematite sleep

Energy rise

Farther than the skies

Infinite sum of everyone

Shamanic divination

Universal forum

Aquarius the merriest

Among the blanketing void

Star shriek

Knees weak

Stare up and wide

A vision decided

One and all

Matter in the small

Connect to the rest

Brain expansion

Antenna to your avatar

The nebula shines inside

RAVAGE

Led astray by the hand
On a thorough demand
Blackmail is the scent of my feeding
Keep quiet and still
The worms are all shrill
But go on running when it's over
Do not scream or I'll grab
The mossy cement slab
And silence you forever

You are worthless to me
A bottle in the sea
Salty without a message
The cut will run deep
Through the gauze it will seep
The poison I put inside you
Fear all that is around
Such a discreet sound

Clamor on and no one will hear you
No trust from your folks
Barbie dolls are your jokes
A lie uncovers something not sacred
Ripped all the hair
A stale plastic stare
An image that can't save you

Covered in the dirt
The trees on alert
Finding refuge in the footing of my being
Guilt I have not
A soul long forgot
I am nothing more than you before me

Run now and cry
Dolls and juice on the sly
I will never be forgotten
The more it kills you
The more I feel true
The monster continues its feasting

Pound

Pound.
Fragile.
Break.
Destroy.
Shake.
Find me.
Or don't.
I will find you.
The ground you walk on.
Crumbles and cracks at your displaced meandering.

Conversation

Training wheels
Gum and squeals
Red Converse high tops
Tearing up my heel
Loose gravel betrayal
Fell on a nail
Skinned my knee
Unable to walk with the band-aid

All it takes is a laugh
Blood I can see
A mother's kiss
Daddy calling you a man
The book that calmed
A yellow slicker and a monkey
The healing sting of balm

The day after too
Rocks and skin
I trampled over
I may slip and fall
And hurt again

But mommy and daddy
Are the firm and sturdy
When I need them most

Door

Those with the key sleep idly
Behind the door is in store
A secret placed elegantly
Locksmith of time
Show the sign
Let in those who seek it
Peeping is a hint
A part of a theoretical whole
Miniscule fraction of your soul

Don't you or I
Want to look inside
Or let life on the sly
Reluctant to be responsible
What magic resides
Beyond our eyes
We only know what we sense
The eyes interpret light
Our mind is our sight

Jostle the handle
Walk on in
You can always leave
But you wouldn't want to

Dove Dive

I found the newspaper floating along
The wind kept going but the paper remained
The view of the obituaries inspired a song
It caught on a shoelace and carried on
The tune became clearer as I worked my home
Over the pavement and past the gnomes

The rhythm made me step in a patterned way
Without buds in my ears, I looked insane
I never personally asked them but they got it across
With their eyes, no less, they said I was nuts
What did I see to carry on so merry
No regard for what people thought
A boost of confidence and no one I fought
A local artist died doing what he loved
Sitting on a stool and painting a dove

It said in the fine print his wife would sell it whole
Including the final panicked, violent stroke

I wasn't so giddy for his death you see
For many a year he was a hero to me
But the man in his will
Close to why the Stones are touring still
Donated the painting to a local school
Not just there for paint strokes and canvas

The kids will now see there was no tragedy with he
He was a triumph to the bitter end
Doing what he loved a heavy message he did send
Love what you love and do it in full
Not being yourself will take its toll
Give yourself to something noble and believe in it all
You will be remembered long after your fall

Distraction

They say noise is a distraction
How high they don't consider
Noise is everywhere
You hear it when you blink
You react profusely when you hear a car alarm
Noise is a constant
Why is it never okay to be normal?
Absolute silence is something the deaf
Who are just as typical a person as anyone else
Are allowed to experience
Their perception of life is such that no hearing person
Can even begin to imagine
Is a disabled person a distraction in society
Not particularly, even though they are given unnecessary attention for "standing out"
The thing that slows perception is letting the abnormality be a bane on your existence
Even if the initial thought is flawed by design

Down Time

Arms around your waist
Sweet embrace
Dripping on your thighs
All the sighs
And the sweat we waste

Love in a form
And in addition to
Connecting more true
A spectacle of wet
The moment we met
Our eyes caught each other
Then we knew
We were one even as two

Hair awry
In the bed I lie
Gazing deep in those greens
A beauty I've never seen
In my dreams you existed
Through a door you walked
As though I enlisted
For our wordless talk

Flowing through us
A feeling so thick
Our interaction feels less like a mix
And more like a pair
The passion of love-making
We dually share

Living Sacrifice

Wood intersecting
Grains maligned
Has the suffering of one
Been lost to false dreams
What once encouraged
Restrained and fixed
Now succumbs to the irony
The mass of cretins
Screaming so
Do they know their motives
Or is their salvation
Tenacious to thoughts
Of only the penitent
Belief is their joke
Understanding is their lie

Rush

Play as a team
Say the stars and a stream
Hands held firm and necks soar higher
Whoever rhymes is a liar
Such affirmations easily said

But let's face it
It soothes the head
I feel fresh as a surge
New as a green leaf
And I'm typing away echoes all
At once

Crowding my mind and losing my rhyming
It does matter at stagnation
But free as the mind
If we're unwoven from impossibility and believing in the sea
People, the stars, and even disease

If we're all lost, nature has won
And in the grand scheme
Such complexity must be working

Love is my answer and like most of the real ones
It makes no sense
Then again, not many things do

Dream Cloud

Dream a little dream, boy
Put the grass between your toes
Saddle by and grace the wind
Staring skyward will cure your woes

Life is always moving
You're tired from catching up
Grasping the tail end of it
It's slip'ry as you go

Simplicity in machinery always moving
Nuts and bolts are soothing
With grease stains in your soul
The ever-beating heart doesn't lull

Pump it
The fist you chase so long
Your voice is all that matters
When you push aside the troll

You as your biggest prey
Trembling in the cobwebs
Low as you can get
Dusty, humid in the summer
The puddle in which you lay

But remember, boy
Your little dream is sink or swim
Closing eyes hypnotize
And lead you far from courage

Nature births and nature takes
Human minds spite the wooded earth
Drive deep and spring forward
Hand-in-hand passion makes

Ease

Twisted ease, we fear the pain
So used to misery lost is hope

Unbelievable it seems when a magnificence
Strolls through the pulsing cavity

Do eyes deceive this wondrous force
Or can reality be higher than our eyes

Absolution is what everyone seeks
Answers are buried in soot
But cleanse the soul of hateful spite
And that magnificence is there for the taking

Mama

Fall among the croup
Flee the sake of all who find the key
Sin the fleece, sheer the cheese
Owe to me nothing

Like some cheap wine, open slowly
Secrets at peace
Screaming the pleas
Of course the east
Soar through the wings

Pray to the heavenly
Lead to me total rehearse
This time recluse
Send him the way to the river

Okay, papa
Sin, sin mama
Step in, take charge
Eat away at me

Sanctity

When one life passes on
We say they're in a better place
But who's to say this place is better
Our nightmares might materialize
And haunt us for eternity

Overtaken by sleep, not knowing of tomorrow
Will it be one of blissful light, or an esoteric curse of black
Is there a Heaven
Is there a God
What lies beyond our illusionary life
Could be the answers we've been searching for

Our curiosity is amok as days are spent
Plodding, uncertain of what's to come
Our lives could end now or in a century stern
The way we live may not come full circle
But who's to say this fragility isn't the beginning

Don't be afraid, just welcome change
For the unknown that will come
Is guaranteed to no one that is born
Embrace this moment of uncertainty
Behind which we may never see

ERIN

Steam vent shutter
Rifling through the clutter
Silent prayers they mutter
Reflect empty space
Show what's truly there

Standing up hair
Twilight star bright
Moon glow shatter
Hearing the clatter
Night stalker on my heels
Extended shadows loom
Illumination flume
Dark in my room

Fright is there
Walls keep me scared
No place I run
Hidden from the sun
Goose bumps up my spine
End of the line
Deep sleep

Mask

Dripping polish
Too much to set
Plenty to fall
Puddle in a palm
Hitting the floor
Would ensure
A slip at the touch of a heel

Bend it back
Too little to hide
To hold tight
What little she has
Of life's little insight

Whitewash

Spring through the trees
Revitalized
True resurrection
Winter's havoc tread
Setting a blistered burn

Look at the street
Once swarming with the sublime
Leaving tracks bitterly
Slaves to a cycle
Ousted once the new sun's routine
Flapping and squawk

Musk of the dormant growth
Wind through my hair
Beauty can deceive
But can't fool
If apparent to the face's apex of view

Safe

Wilted but not defeated
Disease and fear wielded
As a defense
Buried deep inside
The true answer
Stubbornly
Accepting the real
Embracing the veil

Torn down, the cloth lays dormant
Love pushed me
Life kept me alive
Unearthing my answer
Even enemies no longer exist
Another person lost on a path I once knew

Body a weak vehicle
Mind a strong shield
Finding steps without the use of feet
My heart the ideal

SANSKRIT

Solidify
Defy my sight
Rise up
Or sink below
Beneath my foot is disregarded
Stare long into the marble swirl
In the distance a being descends
Sanskrit
Talisman of the feeble
Speak to me by way of hand
Much like the deaf drowning in silence
If deafness is all you know
The scurry of a rat bares no likeness to air

Lacking

Saran wrap blues
Suffocation, brand new hue
Desaturate the magistrate
Can't blink or reason or chew
Without the pulse in my eyes

Sore from lack of sleep
Lack of feeling in my thighs
The alarm clock beeps
From the other room only
And he's not waking up

The boy or man who's belly expands
With the chicken grease on his fingers
I'm being a cynic
But it's hard when you can't count to three
I need a pillow and drink
Not the drip, drip, drip of the sink

Tie the third line of this poem to the rest
Okay, the sun governs my wake-up
The point is
Surely you jest!
I've been telling you I'm tired this entire time

Trying to make metaphors like string and a lime
A tangy thread
A delicious straight path
There's my blanket
I'm not too read on the subject

Blanket

Dangerous flow
Mountains of snow
Avalanche
Pine branch
Dread what no one sees
Dare to be
One in the sink
Thrusting forward
Breathe heavily
Dawn will break
Searing and melting it all
Hoards of logs
Burning in a house made of the same
Dredge beneath the gray crystals
Candle light
Midday bright
The sun casting its warmth above and below
Free from the shadows

Wake

Volcanic ire

Veins are on fire

Smoking out my ears

Golden chandeliers

Mask of alchemy

Blackened on the outside

Hollow on the inside

Rocks sky high

Dust miles above the eye

Bury me

Ripping out a tree

Root and soot

Don't rhyme but look the same

Leg is lame

Got to run away

The molten flame

Terrifying nightmare

No time for scare

Self-preservation

Elk reservation

Home taken away

Land in dangerous shade

Spouting noxious

Ending time

Red and Orange

At dawn, the mist from the fog between the mountains created a dizzying array of colors
It reminded me of a soul being shared between two beings
The vibrance and richness of the miniature rainbows
Were the daydreams circulating my synapses
I was communicating with Truth
The answer that lies throughout the universe without words
I could the taste light and see the fresh fruit before me
Bearing the culmination of the precipitation that made it so serene
When I picked up the peach, it was more wet outside than in
The juices sprayed skyward, heavier and dancing through the thick air
Truth smiled back when in my mind I did unto it
My answers laid before me without even having to try

Pristine

Nature's geometry
The snowflakes in their gentle descent patterned flawless
Uniting mosaics

The blanket is white but
They underline the overwhelming infinity
Inside all of living
Packed together and used as weapons by the children
Defying the inner self

They live and die without a second glance from the eye
Covering the dead things

CRYSTAL CASTLE

In the land beyond the sea
Past the infinite fog of mystery
Lies dormant in the mind
A castle without time
Crystal walls upon a listless cloud
An invisible realm where thoughts are allowed
Graceful light shimmering through
A rainbow peers vastly in the uppermost room
Laying nude on one's side an angel resides
A laugh so bountiful one shivers inside
The fears once had were only a lie
Conditioning gone I float beyond
My feet are a distant memory
Glued to the stream sights so extreme
Tears flow freely like rain over leaves
The freedom of flying kept only in dreams
In the land beyond the sea
Past the infinite fog of mystery
My soul is replenished and my mind cleansed
There's nothing to fear when you come to an end

www.ingramcontent.com/pod-product-compliance
Lightning Source LLC
Chambersburg PA
CBHW031411040426
42444CB00005B/516